LEGENDS
OF THE WEST

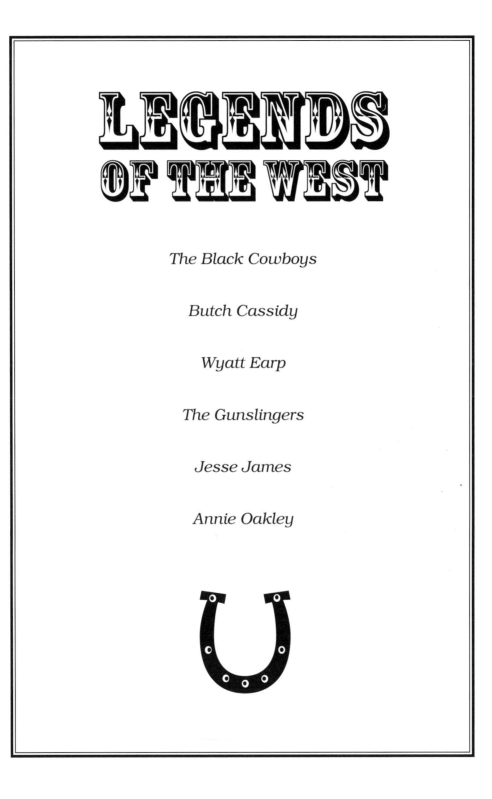

LEGENDS OF THE WEST

BUTCH CASSIDY

John Wukovits

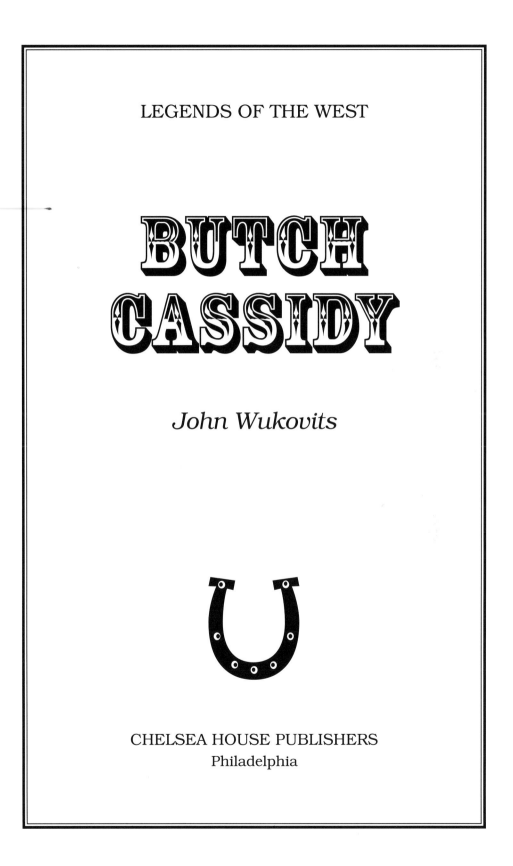

CHELSEA HOUSE PUBLISHERS
Philadelphia

CHELSEA HOUSE PUBLISHERS
Editor-in-Chief : Stephen Reginald
Managing Editor : James D. Gallagher
Production Manager : Pamela Loos
Art Director : Sara Davis
Picture Editor : Judy Hasday
Senior Production Editor : Lisa Chippendale

Staff for **BUTCH CASSIDY**
Cover Design and Digital Illustration : Robert Gerson
Cover Photo Credit : Buffalo Bill Historical Center, Cody, WY;
    Vincent Mercaldo Collection
Picture Researcher : John F. Wukovits
Text Design : Keith Trego

First Printing

1 3 5 7 9 8 6 4 2

Library of Congress Cataloging-in-Publication Data

Wukovits, John F., 1944-
    Butch Cassidy / John Wukovits.
        p. cm. — (Legends of the West)
Includes biographical references and index.
Summary: Follows the life of the man who led the notorious "Wild Bunch" gang,
from his youth as Robert Leroy Parker to his rise to folk-hero status with his part-
ner, the Sundance Kid.
    ISBN 0-7910-3857-2
1. Cassidy, Butch, b. 1866—Juvenile literature. 2. Outlaws—West (U.S.)—Biog-
raphy—Juvenile literature. 3. West (U.S.)—Biography—Juvenile literature. [1.
Cassidy, Butch, b. 1866. 2. Robbers and outlaws.] I. Title. II. Series: Wukovits,
John F., 1944- Legends of the West.
F595.C362W85 1997
364.1'55'092—dc21
[B]   97-13191
                                                                                  CIP
                                                                                   AC

CONTENTS

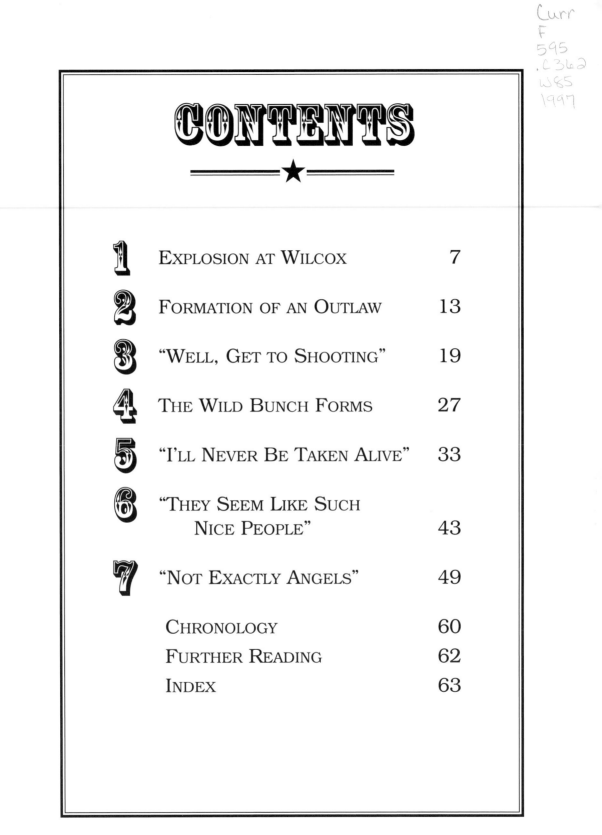

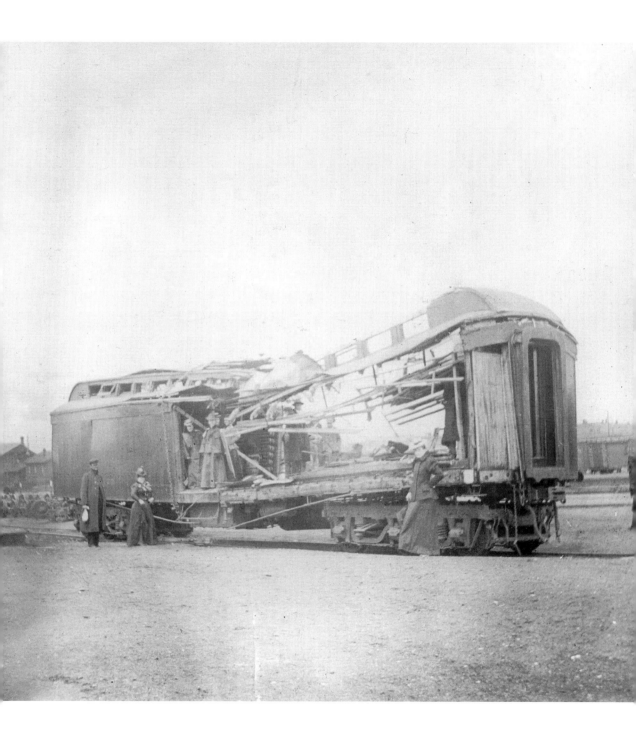

EXPLOSION AT WILCOX

Train engineer W. R. Jones peered into the early morning darkness from the Union Pacific's Overland Flyer as it raced down the tracks on its way to Wilcox, Wyoming. So far the June 2, 1899, run had gone without a hitch and Jones felt confident he would bring his train in on schedule.

All that changed at 2:18 A.M., however. Straining against the darkness to see better, Jones spotted someone waving a red lantern a short distance down the tracks, indicating a problem of some sort. Cursing his bad fortune, Jones hastily applied the brakes to the four-car train. As its wheels screeched against the rails in protest, the train slowed until it came to a complete halt.

Two men, Robert Leroy Parker and Harvey

Butch Cassidy and his gang blew this train car apart trying to open a safe. The gang escaped with $30,000 in the Wilcox train robbery.

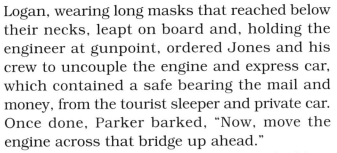

Logan, wearing long masks that reached below their necks, leapt on board and, holding the engineer at gunpoint, ordered Jones and his crew to uncouple the engine and express car, which contained a safe bearing the mail and money, from the tourist sleeper and private car. Once done, Parker barked, "Now, move the engine across that bridge up ahead."

When Jones hesitated, Logan cracked him hard across the face a few times with his revolver, a tactic frequently used by the two bandits. As Parker explained to friends, the two preferred smacking people with the long barrel of a revolver, because "if there's a hero among the passengers or train crew, it's better to hit him across the nose. A man automatically raises his hand to protect his face. It doesn't create a fuss and there's no killin'."

The bleeding engineer guided his train across the bridge, where four other masked men ran to the express car door and warned the clerk inside, E. C. Woodcock, to open up or face harm. When Woodcock refused, the four men placed a few sticks of dynamite near the door, lit the fuses, then rushed away a short distance. A loud explosion ripped a hole in the express car door with such force that, as one of the crew later recalled, "Woodcock was stunned and had to be taken from the car."

The outlaws rushed through the shattered door into the car, where they piled more dynamite near their objective—the safe and its valuable contents. As all six thieves watched alongside the tracks, a second explosion tore apart the safe. However, after the blast, the outlaws stared toward the sky in horror as a cloud of shredded greenbacks littered the heavens. Rather than applying the correct amount of

Harvey Logan, a member of Butch's gang, was a crack shot.

dynamite without damaging what it held, the men had used so much that the safe's contents now blanketed the countryside.

In almost comical fashion the six scurried around the tracks and surrounding area picking up whatever remained of their loot, some of which had been stained a deep red by demolished crates of raspberries. Jones and the crew did not know whether to laugh or cry as they witnessed six armed, masked men dash from spot to spot chasing bits of greenbacks.

When the outlaws had finished, they mounted their horses and hurried away with the $30,000 they were fortunate enough to retrieve. Jones, Woodcock, and the others recoupled the remaining parts of the train, pulled into Wilcox two hours behind schedule, and alerted authorities to the robbery. While they could not identify any of the armed men, they pointed out that generally, "they appeared not to want to hurt anyone and were quite sociable." An outlaw even "asked one of the boys for a chew of tobacco."

Sheriff Joseph Hazen quickly assembled a posse and set out after Parker and the gang. After picking up their trail, Hazen and his men hotly pursued the outlaws for miles, exchanging gunfire along the way. Even though the bandits were able to stop and pick up fresh horses three times, they could not shake the determined Hazen. Frustrated, the outlaws' leader took them into a small canyon near Teapot Creek, about thirty miles north of Caspar, Wyoming.

Hazen followed hot on the heels of his quarry, and within minutes the peaceful canyon thundered with the sound of gunfire and the zings of ricocheting bullets. Sheltering behind boulders for protection, Parker and his men kept the posse at bay with a withering barrage, but nothing seemed to shake their pursuers.

Even the loss of their leader did not slow the posse. When Logan, one of the region's most accurate shots, mortally wounded the sheriff, the other lawmen continued to fire well into the night. As dawn neared, however, they noticed that return fire from the criminals had slackened, and when they rushed in with the early morning daylight they discovered that Parker, Logan, and the rest had slipped through their lines during the night and escaped.

Saddened by the dual blow of losing their leader and the outlaws, the posse returned home. Once again, Robert Leroy Parker—better known to history as Butch Cassidy—had successfully eluded the law's reach and safely extricated his gang, nicknamed the Wild Bunch, from harm.

The Wilcox robbery typified most of Cassidy's operations, whether directed against banks or express cars. He never acted alone, and he normally organized the heists. In fact, some accounts doubt whether he was even present during the Wilcox operation, though all agree that he at least planned the affair.

Over the years, stories spread that although Butch Cassidy stole money, he hated violence and tried not to harm anyone. This image of Cassidy as a harmless individual who simply inconvenienced other people by taking their money may make for pleasant reading, but it ignores the harsh reality. Cassidy may not have injured anyone at Wilcox, but because of the robbery which Cassidy orchestrated, Woodcock left with a cracked skull, the Hazen family had to bury Joseph, the Union Pacific had to replace damaged railroad cars, businesses and individuals lost money, railroad crew and posse members faced danger and death, and families fretted for the safety of loved ones. Cassidy was far from being a harmless individual, and his actions created havoc wherever he lived.

Formation
of an Outlaw

Robert Leroy Parker came from sturdy stock. His father, Max, arrived in the United States from England with his Mormon parents. The Parkers traveled to Iowa City with plans to purchase a wagon and head west, but with such a great flood of settlers gushing across the Mississippi River, wagons were either unavailable or too costly. So like other poorer families hoping to find a better life in the West, the determined group piled its few belongings onto a two-wheeled handcart and pulled it the entire 1,300 miles to the Mormon community of Beaver in southern Utah.

Max worked as a mail carrier and eventually married a Mormon girl, Annie Gillies. Their first of 13 children—Robert Leroy—was born on April 13, 1866. As if a large family was not enough—for other children appeared in rapid

Robert Parker, aka Butch Cassidy, grew up in the pleasant surroundings of a small Utah town.

order—the stubborn and energetic Robert gave his parents all they could handle. He hated attending both school and church and would do practically anything to avoid either. One of his sisters recalled that while the rest of the family rode into town for Sunday services, "If he could find some chore—any chore—that needed attention, he stayed home to take care of it. Any excuse was convenient."

On the other hand, the rebellious boy developed traits which endeared him to many of the families in the area and which he carried into adulthood. He flashed a constant smile, and he loved children. Annie explained how her Robert "made a fuss over kids, and they loved him, whether they were our own, our relatives', or neighbors'. There was always room on his horse for as many as could scramble up. If they were little, he'd put them all on and lead the horse."

What transforms a charming youth bearing a gracious smile into one of the West's most infamous outlaws? Some accounts point to two events in his early years that nudged Robert toward the path he eventually adopted. When Robert was 13, his father filed a claim for a promising section of land in the area. A problem arose when a second settler put in his own claim for the same land. The local Mormon bishop was asked to decide the dispute, and his ruling in favor of the second man enraged Robert. Already estranged from his parents' religion, the teenager claimed that the bishop cheated his father out of the land to punish Max for not regularly attending church and for smoking.

At approximately the same time, Robert rode into nearby Circleville to purchase supplies at the general store. Finding the store closed, and hating to travel the long distance home empty-

handed, Robert broke in, selected the needed materials, and left an IOU note on the counter for the amount. Robert then rode home, confident the store owner would honor the note.

He was wrong. The businessman swore out a complaint. Though the matter was settled out of court, Robert added the legal system to his short list of distasteful institutions. If a man's word was not good enough for the law, the law was not good enough for him, reasoned Robert.

By his 18th birthday, the young man had matured into a capable ranch hand. Although Robert was small at 5 feet 9 inches and 155 pounds, his skill with a horse and rope, combined with his pleasant personality and sense of humor, made him popular with other hands.

Although Butch was not very big, his skill with horses and with a lariat made him a good ranch hand.

Robert learned most of his cowboy skills from another ranch hand. Mike Cassidy not only taught the youth the finer points of riding and roping, but gave him a pistol and saddle. Robert idolized Mike and frequently could be found in his company. This growing friendship worried Annie, who heard rumors of Cassidy's involvement in stealing horses and cattle.

Sadly, the rumors were true. Mike Cassidy headed an elaborate operation that stole the animals, then transported the horses and cattle into a wild region of southeastern Utah frequented by outlaws. Robert participated in these illegal activities, which obviously irritated local ranchers. In 1884 the ranchers filed charges against a group of men, including Cassidy and Robert, but to help his cohorts, most of whom had already fled the region, Robert signed a document swearing that he was to blame. He then quickly departed Beaver before the authorities could arrest him and headed for Robber's Roost, a desolate region in southeastern Utah. Out of respect for Mike, who found safety in Mexico, Robert changed his last name to Cassidy.

Hand in hand with Robert's fondness for criminal activities was his continued development of admirable characteristics. George Streeter, who worked with Robert for two years in the mid-1880s, claimed that not only could Robert ride around a tree at top speed and still carve a three-inch circle into it with bullets from his revolver, but that the constantly smiling Cassidy "was the best natured man I ever saw and he would never stand for anyone molesting me."

Another cowhand, John F. Kelly, worked with Cassidy in Montana in 1886. One day Cassidy asked Kelly to loan him 25 dollars so he could travel to Butte, Montana. He promised to repay him as soon as he could. Kelly, who enjoyed riding the range with the young man, handed over the money without actually believing that his companion would make good on his promise.

Within one year, though, Kelly had more than his money back when Cassidy mailed the repayment. "When I opened [the letter] one hundred dollars in cash fell out. The letter said simply, 'If you don't know how I got this, you will soon learn someday.'"

Those final words proved prophetic, as Cassidy developed a reputation in the 1880s and 1890s in the West, not for kindness and trust, but for criminal activity. The young Robert Leroy Parker, now called Robert Cassidy, had turned to the occupation in which he would excel for the remainder of his life—stealing money.

"Well, Get to Shooting"

After scurrying out of Utah, Cassidy briefly worked in a Colorado mine. However, this way of living quickly lost its appeal to the restless youth, who yearned for excitement and action. He found it back in familiar Robber's Roost, where he and another drifter named Matt Warner joined a gang specializing in train and bank robberies headed by the three McCarty brothers—Bill, Tom, and George.

Cassidy's initial venture into train robbing started in frustration and, similar to his subsequent Wilcox operation, ended in almost comical fashion. On November 3, 1887, the five members stopped a train and threatened to shoot the express company messenger, who was in charge of money and valuables—unless he opened the safe. However, the brash railroad worker unexpectedly refused. Flustered, the five held a speedy meeting and concluded that

Robber's Roost—the rocky hideout of Butch Cassidy and his gang.

Tom McCarty and his two brothers joined Butch on a spree of bank and train robberies in Colorado.

a safe was not worth killing someone over. One of the five wondered about robbing the passengers, but already thwarted by the stubborn clerk, the five jumped back on their horses and rode away empty-handed.

The men regained sufficient nerve to attempt a second robbery a little over a year later. On March 30, 1889, Cassidy walked into Denver's First National Bank with Tom McCarty, holding a bottle of clear liquid in his hand. The two approached the bank's president, warned him that the liquid was highly explosive nitro-glycerin, and ordered him to open the safe or they would blow up the bank. The shaken officer did as he was told, and within 15 minutes Cassidy and McCarty galloped away from Denver, minus one bottle of harmless water but $21,000 richer.

The big score in Denver whetted their appetites for more robberies. Only three months later, on June 24, 1889, the five hit the San Miguel Valley Bank in Telluride, Colorado, in what a Denver newspaper described as "one of the boldest affairs of the kind ever known in southern Colorado."

For two days before the robbery the gang roamed Telluride and drank whiskey in its saloons to gain information about the bank. They learned that two men worked inside—a clerk and Mr. Painter, the cashier. When Painter left the bank on an errand one afternoon, the gang made its move.

While Tom McCarty watched the horses and Cassidy protected the front door, Matt Warner stepped inside, strode directly to the clerk and, according to the newspaper, "grabbed him around the neck, pulling his face down on the desk, at the same time admonishing the surprised official to keep quiet on pain of instant death." He then yelled to his companions, "Come on, boys, it's all right," and watched the clerk while McCarty and Cassidy stuffed cash into canvas bags.

When they finished, Warner released the frightened clerk, who fell in a heap on the floor. Warner stared disgustedly at the man and said, "I have a notion to shoot you anyway for being such a coward." However, Warner spared the man and joined his comrades outside.

With almost $22,000 in greenbacks, the gang rode to Keystone Hill just outside of town, where another member waited with fresh horses. A posse chased after them, but the outlaws escaped after tying branches to a horse and sending it at a gallop toward their pursuers. The posse lost so much time calming their frightened horses that it never caught up to the gang again.

The McCarty gang broke up the next spring when the three brothers headed for Oregon. Cassidy traveled to Wyoming, where he worked as a cowhand and a butcher in a Rock Springs meat market. Though no one knows for sure, it is likely he picked up his nickname, Butch, during the early 1890s because of his occupation at Rock Springs.

Whatever legal jobs he held, Butch Cassidy always had his hand in some shady business as well, either in the planning stage or in the actual deed itself. While he did not participate in robbing any banks for a few years, he and a friend, Al Hainer, purchased a ranch on Horse Creek near Lander, Wyoming. Though the two had no visible means of support, for Cassidy never held any job for very long, they always seemed to have money to purchase supplies for their ranch or to support spending sprees in the town's stores and saloons. As other local ranchers had seen their cattle and horses mysteriously disappear, suspicion fell on the two newcomers living along Horse Creek. Angry ranch owners implemented a plan to trap Cassidy and Hainer.

Billy Nucher, a known horse thief, sold three horses to Butch. Though he was suspicious of the seller, Cassidy purchased the horses when Nucher swore the animals had not been stolen. Shortly after the deal, however, a rancher named Otto Franc filed a complaint against Hainer and Cassidy for stealing his horses, forcing the two to ride into hiding near Auburn, Wyoming.

Deputy Sheriff Bob Calverly set out in pur-

suit and quickly pinpointed their hideout. Since he heard that the daughter of a local rancher was staying with the fugitives, Calverly simply waited in town until the girl showed up to claim mail, then learned from her exactly where the wanted men were staying. Calverly and another lawman rode out to a saw mill where Hainer worked and arrested him, then headed for the

The McCarty gang's robbery at the San Miguel Valley Bank in Telluride, Colorado, was described by newspaper accounts as "one of the boldest affairs of the kind ever known." The gang got away with $22,000.

cabin where Butch was.

On April 8, 1892, Calverly cautiously approached the shack. As he later recalled, "I told Butch I had a warrant for him, but Cassidy shouted back, 'Well, get to shooting.'" As bullets flew in all directions, Calverly advanced until the two could almost touch each other.

"I put the barrel of my revolver almost to his stomach, but it missed three times but owing to the fact that there was another man between us, he failed to hit me," Calverly said. "The fourth time I snapped the gun it went off and the bullet hit him in the upper part of the forehead and felled him. I then had him and he made no further resistance."

In June 1893 Butch Cassidy and Al Hainer went on trial for stealing Franc's three horses, but a jury found both men not guilty. Otto Franc swore out a second complaint, this time charging only Butch with stealing his horses, which led Cassidy to wonder whether his partner had made a deal with the law to give information against Butch in exchange for his freedom. When a jury found Cassidy guilty in this trial, Butch was convinced Hainer had turned him in.

Settlers in the West considered stealing horses such a serious offense that a man could be hanged for it, but Cassidy received the relatively light sentence of two years at hard labor. On July 15, 1894, Butch Cassidy entered the Laramie City, Wyoming, penitentiary to begin what would turn out to be 18 months of confinement. As he later explained, the harsh reality that he was cut off from society hit him the moment "the cell door closed. I was then completely broken."

The free-spirited Cassidy hated life behind thick walls. He tried to pass the time by constantly exercising, but being locked away with hardened criminals embittered him even more. He claimed later that while he was a criminal before entering prison, his experience at Laramie City hardened him into an outlaw.

Cassidy received his freedom on January 19, 1896, after making a deal with Wyoming's governor. Supposedly he wrote to Governor William A. Richards, "If you will pardon me, I will promise to leave the state of Wyoming alone." Since Cassidy had already served much of his time, Richards agreed to the deal.

Cassidy had no intention of either living up to the deal or of abandoning his criminal ways. He resolved to be "the most dreaded, most hunted and surely the most elusive outlaw that either North or South America have had to contend with as yet."

Butch headed straight for another favorite outlaw hideout, Brown's Hole, near the Utah-Idaho border, where he formed a gang of outlaws that, for the remainder of the century, would frustrate law officers and enrage railroad and bank executives. Butch Cassidy and his gang, the Wild Bunch, were ready to pounce upon an unsuspecting world.

The Wild Bunch Forms

Butch Cassidy wasted little time gathering a group of ruthless thieves, for he now planned to go after the bigger payoffs lying in the safes of the more prosperous banks and in the express trains that transported payroll sacks and bank money to and from the East. First he carefully selected three locations to which he and his gang could flee for shelter after each job. In addition to Robber's Roost, he chose the barren locales provided by Brown's Hole near the Colorado-Wyoming border, where he and another member of the Wild Bunch, Elza Lay, built a cabin on a rocky elevation.

The third spot, Hole-in-the-Wall, carries a name that frequently appears in stories told of the West. A steep cliff stretching for 50 miles cuts across central Wyoming and forms a rocky barricade for the caverns, canyons, and ravines tucked securely inside its confines. Only one narrow, bumpy trail punctures the fortress,

Harvey "Kid Curry" Logan was one of the regular members of Butch Cassidy's gang.

An educated, married man, Elza Lay was the least likely criminal among the "Wild Bunch." He also was Butch Cassidy's closest friend.

meaning that a gang running from the law could easily flee inside, then prevent their pursuers from entering by posting men to guard the solitary entrance.

There were usually several different gangs milling about the area, either hiding from the law, preparing for their next operation, or both, but the group that became most famous in the annals of the West is Butch Cassidy's Wild Bunch.

Labeled Wild Bunch by fellow outlaws and by the press because they lived reckless lives, the gang rarely consisted of the same individuals for each robbery. Cassidy remained firmly in command even though he frequently asked other members for their advice and encouraged his men to speak their mind about future heists. While Cassidy disliked violence—preferring to shoot at posses' horses rather than at the pursuers riding them—and claimed on a number of occasions that "I have never killed a man," some of his cohorts readily resorted to the gun whenever needed. Mostly in their mid-thirties, some men joined for one robbery, took their money, and were never seen again. Others drifted in and out two or three different times.

A core of outlaws, however, rode with Cassidy with such regularity that they are regarded as the gang's members. After Cassidy, the most famous was the handsome, immaculately-dressed Henry Longbaugh, called the Sundance Kid because he came from Sundance, Wyoming. Longbaugh could mesmerize people—especially women—with one glance from his dazzling blue-gray eyes that stared out from beneath sandy hair. So quiet that he rarely muttered more than a few words, Longbaugh seldom allowed a smile to crease his elegant face. An

expert marksman, Longbaugh possessed a trig-
ger temper that often landed him in trouble.

Elza Lay was another expert marksman and
horse rider. Perhaps Cassidy's closest friend
among the Wild Bunch, the educated Lay least
fit the image of a ruthless criminal. Deeply in
love with his wife and the father of two daughters, Lay eventually studied geology under a
famed Yale University professor and performed
significant work in that academic field. Cassidy
labeled him "the educated member" of the group.

Harvey Logan, better known as Kid Curry,
had an even nastier temper than the Sundance
Kid. Cassidy claimed Curry was "the bravest
man I ever knew," because Curry had absolute-
ly no fear of anyone or anything. He cared little about his own life and thought nothing of
taking risks that others might avoid.

The Tall Texan, Ben Kilpatrick, sported looks
that belied his happy-go-lucky attitude. A gross-
ly disfigured left eye marred an otherwise jovial
face, but despite the imperfection, women
warmed to Kilpatrick's pleasant demeanor. He
loved to play practical jokes, but the skilled
shooter could also quickly turn to his gun when
needed. To hide the fact that he could not read,
Kilpatrick always ordered ham and beans in any
saloon he entered.

Some of Cassidy's companions from earlier
days also appeared with the Wild Bunch, such
as Matt Warner, Henry Meek, who had worked
with Butch as a mule skinner, and Bill Carver.
Possibly the most unusual, though, was Etta
Place, a striking woman with reddish-brown hair,
brown eyes, and a captivating smile who accompanied the Sundance Kid through most of his
adventures. Place loved the outdoors, reveled
in dashing off to different parts of the country,

Pinkerton's National Detective Agency.

FOUNDED BY ALLAN PINKERTON, 1850.

OFFICES.

ROBT. A. PINKERTON, New York.
WM. A. PINKERTON, Chicago. } Principals.

GEO. D. BANGS, General Manager, New York.
ALLAN PINKERTON, Assistant General Manager, New York.

JOHN CORNISH, Gen'l Sup't., Eastern Division, New York.
EDWARD S. GAYLOR, Gen'l Sup't., Middle Division, Chicago.
JAMES McPARLAND, Gen'l Supt., Western Division, Denver.

Attorneys:—GUTHRIE, CRAVATH & HENDERSON, New York.

DENVER,   Opera House Block.
J. C. FRASER, Sup't.
NEW YORK,   67 Broadway
BOSTON,   30 Court Street
PHILADELPHIA, 441 Chestnut Street
MONTREAL, Merchants Bank Building
CHICAGO,   Fifth Avenue
ST. PAUL,   Germania Bank Building
ST. LOUIS,   Wainwright Building
KANSAS CITY,   622 Main Street
PORTLAND, ORE. Marquam Block
SEATTLE, WASH. Bailey Block
SAN FRANCISCO, Crocker Building

TELEPHONE CONNECTION.

REPRESENTING THE AMERICAN BANKERS' ASSOCIATION.

$4,000.00 REWARD.

CIRCULAR No. 2.

DENVER, Colo., January 24th, 1902.

THE FIRST NATIONAL BANK OF WINNEMUCCA, Nevada, a member of THE AMERICAN BANKERS' ASSOCIATION, was robbed of $32,640 at the noon hour, September 19th, 1900, by three men who entered the bank and "held up" the cashier and four other persons. Two of the robbers carried revolvers and a third a Winchester rifle. They compelled the five persons to go into the inner office of the bank while the robbery was committed.

At least $31,000 was in $20 gold coin; $1,200 in $5 and $10 gold coin; the balance in currency, including one $50 bill.

Since the issuance of our first circular, dated Denver, Colo., May 15th, 1901, it has been positively determined that two of the men who committed this robbery were:

1. GEORGE PARKER, alias "BUTCH" CASSIDY, alias GEORGE CASSIDY, alias INGERFIELD.
2. HARRY LONGBAUGH, alias "KID" LONGBAUGH, alias HARRY ALONZO, alias "THE SUNDANCE KID."

PARKER and LONGBAUGH are members of the HARVEY LOGAN alias "KID" CURRY band of bank and train (express) "hold up" robbers.

For the arrest, detention and surrender to an authorized officer of the State of Nevada of each or any one of the men who robbed the FIRST NATIONAL BANK OF WINNEMUCCA, the following rewards are offered:

BY THE FIRST NATIONAL BANK OF WINNEMUCCA: $1,000 for each robber.
Also 25 per cent., in proportionate shares, on all money recovered.

BY THE AMERICAN BANKERS' ASSOCIATION: $1,000 for each robber.
This reward to be paid on proper identification of either PARKER or LONGBAUGH.

Persons furnishing information leading to the arrest of either or all of the robbers will be entitled to share in the reward.

The outlaws, whose photographs, descriptions and histories appear on this circular MAY ATTEMPT TO CIRCULATE or be in possession of the following described NEW INCOMPLETE BANK NOTES of the NATIONAL BANK OF MONTANA and THE AMERICAN NATIONAL BANK, both of HELENA, MONT., which were stolen by members of the HARVEY LOGAN, alias "KID" CURRY BAND, from the GREAT NORTHERN RAILWAY EXPRESS No. 3, near Wagner, Mont., July 3rd, 1901, by "hold up" methods.

$40,000. INCOMPLETE NEW BANK NOTES OF NATIONAL BANK OF MONTANA (Helena, Montana), $24,000 of which was in ten dollar bills and $16,000 of which was in twenty dollar bills.

Serial Number 1201 to 2000 inclusive;
Government Number–Y 934349 to 935148 inclusive;
Charter Number 5671.

$500. INCOMPLETE BANK NOTES OF AMERICAN NATIONAL BANK (Helena, Montana), $300 of which was in ten dollar bills and $200 of which was in twenty dollar bills.

Serial Number 3423 to 3432 inclusive;
Government Number V–662761 to V–662770 inclusive;
Charter Number 4396.

THESE INCOMPLETE BANK NOTES LACKED THE SIGNATURES OF THE PRESIDENTS AND CASHIERS OF THE BANKS NAMED, AND MAY BE CIRCULATED WITHOUT SIGNATURES OR WITH FORGED SIGNATURES.

Chiefs of Police, Sheriffs, Marshals and Constables receiving copy of this circular should furnish a copy of the above described stolen currency to banks, bankers, money brokers, gambling houses, pool room keepers and request their co-operation in the arrest of any person or persons presenting any of these bills.

THE UNITED STATES TREASURY DEPARTMENT REFUSES TO REDEEM THESE STOLEN UNSIGNED OR IMPROPERLY SIGNED NOTES.

Officers are warned to have sufficient assistance and be fully armed, when attempting to arrest either of these outlaws, as they are always heavily armed, and will make a determined resistance before submitting to arrest, not hesitating to kill, if necessary.

Foreign ministers and consuls receiving copy of this circular are respectfully requested to give this circular to the police of their city or district.
Postmasters receiving this circular are requested to place same in hands of reliable Police official, Marshal, Constable, Sheriff or Deputy, or a Peace officer.

Below appear the photographs, descriptions and histories of GEORGE PARKER, alias "BUTCH" CASSIDY, alias GEORGE CASSIDY, alias INGERFIELD and HARRY LONGBAUGH alias HARRY ALONZO.

GEORGE PARKER.
First photograph taken July 11, 1894.

GEORGE PARKER.
Last photograph taken Nov. 21, 1900.

Name.......George Parker, alias "Butch" Cassidy, alias George Cassidy, alias Ingerfield.
Nationality.......American
Occupation.......Cowboy; rustler
Criminal Occupation.......Bank robber and highwayman, cattle and horse thief
Age..36 yrs. (1901)...Height....5 feet 9 in
Weight..165 lbs.....Build....Medium
Complexion..Light...Color of Hair..Flaxen
Eyes....Blue....Mustache..Sandy, if any
Remarks:—Two cut scars back of head, small scar under left eye, small brown mole calf of leg. "Butch" Cassidy is known as a criminal principally in Wyoming, Utah, Idaho, Colorado and Nevada and has served time in Wyoming State penitentiary at Laramie for grand larceny, but was pardoned January 19th, 1896.

HARRY LONGBAUGH.
Photograph taken Nov. 21, 1900.

Name.......Harry Longbaugh, alias "Kid" Longbaugh, alias Harry Alonzo alias Frank Jones, alias Frank Boyd, alias the "Sundance Kid"
Nationality.......Swedish-American..Occupation.......Cowboy; rustler
Criminal Occupation.......Highwayman, bank burglar, cattle and horse thief
Age......35 years....Height....5 feet 10 in
Weight...165 to 175 lbs....Build.....Good
Eyes....Blue or gray.....Complexion....Medium
Mustache or Beard.....(if any), natural color brown, reddish tinge
Features.....Grecian type....Nose.....Rather long
Color of Hair.....Natural color brown, may be dyed; combs it pompadour.
IS BOW-LEGGED AND HIS FEET FAR APART.
Remarks:—Harry Longbaugh served 18 months in jail at Sundance, Cook Co., Wyoming, when a boy, for horse stealing. In December, 1892, Harry Longbaugh, Bill Madden and Henry Bass "held up" a Great Northern train at Malta, Montana. Bass and Madden were tried for this crime, convicted and sentenced to 10 and 14 years respectively; Longbaugh escaped and since has been a fugitive. June 28, 1897, under the name of Frank Jones, Longbaugh participated with Harvey Logan, alias Curry, Tom Day and Walter Putney, in the Belle Fourche, South Dakota, bank robbery. All were arrested, but Longbaugh and Harvey Logan escaped from jail at Deadwood, October 31, the same year. Longbaugh has not since been arrested.

We also publish below a photograph, history and description of CAMILLA HANKS, alias O. C. HANKS, alias CHARLEY JONES, alias "DEAF" CHARLEY, who may be found in the company of either PARKER or CASSIDY or LONGBAUGH, alias ALONZO, and for whom a proportionate amount of a $5,000.00 Reward is offered by the GREAT NORTHERN EXPRESS COMPANY upon arrest and conviction for participation in the Great Northern (Railway) Express robbery near Wagner, Mont., July 3rd, 1901.

CAMILLA HANKS.
Photograph taken 1892.

Name.......O. C. Hanks, alias Camilla Hanks, alias Charley Jones, alias Deaf Charley
Nationality.....American.....Occupation.....Cowboy
Criminal Occupation.........Train robber; an ex-convict
Age....38 years (1901)....Height....5 feet 10 in
Weight....156 lbs......Build......Good
Complexion.....Sandy.....Color of Hair.....Auburn
Eyes.....Blue.....Mustache or Beard....(if any), natural color sandy
Remarks:—Scar from burn, size 25c piece, on right forearm. Small scar right leg, above ankle. Mole near right nipple. Leans his head slightly to the left. Somewhat deaf. Raised at Yorktown, Texas, fugitive from there charged with rape; also wanted in New Mexico on charge of murder. Arrested in Teton County, Montana, 1892, and sentenced to 10 years in the penitentiary at Deer Lodge, for holding up Northern Pacific train near Big Timber, Montana. Released April 30th, 1901.

HARVEY LOGAN, alias "KID" CURRY, referred to in our first circular issued from Denver on May 15, 1901, is now under arrest at Knoxville, Tenn., charged with shooting two police officers who were attempting his arrest.
BEN KILPATRICK, alias JOHN ARNOLD, alias "THE TALL TEXAN" of Concho County, Texas, another member of the "Harvey Logan band" of outlaws, was arrested at St. Louis, Mo., on November 8th, 1901, tried, convicted and sentenced to 15 years imprisonment for participation in the robbery of the GREAT NORTHERN EXPRESS COMPANY, near Wagner, Mont.
WILLIAM CARVER, alias "BILL" CARVER, of Sonora, Sutton County, Texas, another member of this band, was killed at Sonora, Texas, April 2nd, 1901, by Sheriff E. S. Briant, while resisting arrest on charge of murder.
IN CASE OF AN ARREST immediately notify PINKERTON'S NATIONAL DETECTIVE AGENCY at the nearest of the above listed offices.
Or
JOHN C. FRASER,
Resident Sup't., DENVER, COLO.

Pinkerton's National Detective Agency,
Opera House Block, Denver, Colo.

requested to give this circular to the police of their city or district.
Police official, Marshal, Constable, Sheriff or Deputy, or a Peace officer.

Pinkerton detectives, hired by railroad and bank owners, hunted the Wild Bunch for many years. This is a circular the agency prepared and circulated in Colorado around 1902.

and sought a life of pleasure and ease.

Butch planned one of their earliest holdups to help Matt Warner, who had been arrested for a double murder and needed money to hire defense lawyers. Butch selected a bank in Montpelier, Idaho, then worked on a nearby ranch while he scouted the bank and surrounding area.

They struck on August 13, 1896. While Meek held the horses, Cassidy and Elza Lay casually strolled into the bank near closing time and, at gunpoint, demanded the bank's money. After grabbing over $7,000 in greenbacks and gold, the trio raced out of town to get a head start on the posse that was sure to follow. They easily outdistanced the law by switching to fresh horses stocked at Montpelier Pass.

Though Cassidy hired a superb legal team of four lawyers, headed by noted attorney Douglas V. Preston, a jury convicted Warner of both charges. However, Preston's eloquent words convinced the judge to sentence Warner to a surprisingly light term of five years.

Butch, however, was after bigger pickings, particularly those offered by trains and business payrolls. After waiting an entire week for the Denver & Rio Grande train to pull into Castle Gate, Utah, he and Lay struck on April 21, 1897. As the paymaster for the Pleasant Valley Coal Company stepped off with the company payroll, Butch walked up to the worker, stuck his revolver into the man's ribs, and ran off with the satchel of money. Though a posse followed, Butch and Lay evaded them by hiding behind a shed while the lawmen galloped by, then riding off in the opposite direction. The two reached Brown's Hole with what was to them a disappointing $8,800.

The money, though insignificant to Cassidy and Lay, meant far more to others. Since Cassidy had selected a train for this operation, he came to the attention of powerful businessmen back east. Railroad magnates were in business to make money, not have it stolen, and they demanded that the guilty men be found and punished. From now on not only the law, but private detectives hired by railroad owners, doggedly hounded the Wild Bunch.

5

"I'll Never Be Taken Alive"

C assidy and Lay worked as cowboys on a New Mexico ranch for a year while the law searched for them. In fact, Cassidy exhibited such skill as a ranch hand that the manager promoted him to foreman.

The Wild Bunch next struck on July 11, 1899, near Folsom, New Mexico. Though they rode off with $30,000, the gang paid a heavy price when a posse doggedly tracked and caught up to them. Three lawmen died in the ensuing gun battle, but Butch lost his most capable planner and friend, Elza Lay, when a marshal's bullet badly wounded the robber. The rest of the Wild Bunch had to head out without their companion, who was captured, tried, and sentenced to a long term in prison.

The arrest of Elza Lay ushered in a string of

The Wild Bunch: (front, l-r) Harry Longbaugh (The Sundance Kid), Ben Kilpatrick, Butch Cassidy; (back) Will Carver, Harvey Logan. The gang had the photograph taken as a joke, but copies of the photo soon hung on every lawman's office wall in the West.

efforts by railroad owners and the law to finally eliminate the Wild Bunch. Disgusted with the wave of lawlessness that threatened their livestock and money, local ranchers had already launched one organized effort to chase criminals out of Brown's Hole and Hole-in-the-Wall. While the raids worked for only a short time, they informed Cassidy and the rest that their lawless sprees would be challenged.

The main source of opposition came from executives at the Union Pacific, who lost not only money but also customer confidence whenever Cassidy or other gangs successfully hit their trains. Following Cassidy's Wilcox heist, the Union Pacific hired the nation's premier private investigation firm, the Pinkerton National Detective Agency, to wipe out the gangs and once more make the trains safe for all customers.

In addition to hiring expert detectives, the Pinkerton Agency employed every modern advancement available. Whereas outlaws used to be able to rob a bank or a train and then disappear, technological improvements such as the telegraph and telephone spread news of any robbery with such speed throughout the entire West that law officers and Pinkerton men knew about it within minutes and could almost immediately send out posses. The Pinkerton Agency started to draw an ever-tightening noose around Butch Cassidy and other wanted outlaws.

Wild Bunch member Bob Meek had carelessly ridden out of Brown's Hole on a personal matter when he was seized, tried, and sentenced to a lengthy jail term. An alarmed Butch, who already had enough money to live comfortably, hired a lawyer to investigate whether an amnesty deal could be made with the governor of Utah, but the politician refused to bargain.

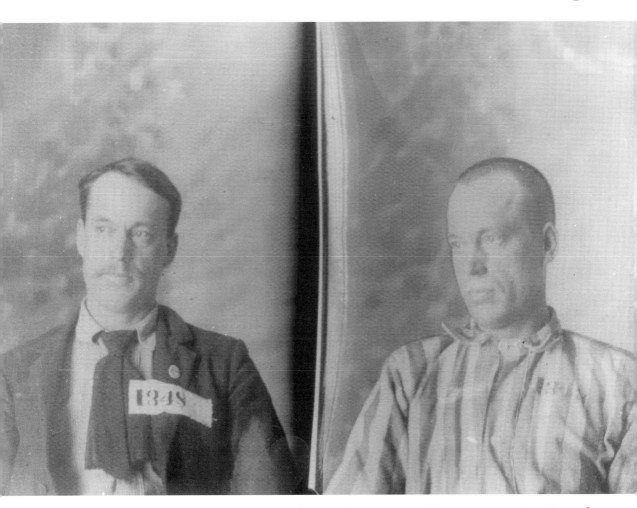

After serving a prison term for his crimes, Elza Lay lived a quiet life in Wyoming, conducting geological experiments in the West.

However, anxious to remove a huge thorn from their side, Union Pacific executives offered Butch an attractive package. The deal included, among other items, hiring him as an express guard at an extremely high salary and dropping all charges against him if he agreed to stop raiding their trains. Butch accepted the offer and rode to the site of a prearranged meeting, but the railroad officials failed to show up. Thinking he had been double-crossed, Cassidy ended his brief flirtation with the law.

Unknown to the outlaw, railroad executives

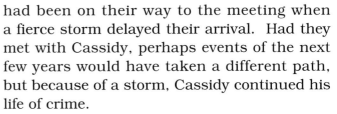

had been on their way to the meeting when a fierce storm delayed their arrival. Had they met with Cassidy, perhaps events of the next few years would have taken a different path, but because of a storm, Cassidy continued his life of crime.

Butch robbed another train, which set in motion further steps by the railroad to hunt him down. The Union Pacific collected the finest trackers and marksmen in the West, supplied them with the latest high-powered rifles, and placed them on a specially-designed train that could quickly transport them wherever necessary. Pulled by the mightiest engine produced, the train contained living quarters for the lawmen and horse stalls for their swift animals. Should Cassidy strike, lawmen who had no qualms about killing their quarry would be in hot pursuit.

Until this point, Butch had not had trouble evading the law. His amiable nature insured that wherever he rode, friends would shield him, but how long could that last? The Sundance Kid repeatedly vowed, "I'll never be taken alive," and Cassidy swore he would never return to prison, so they started to consider other places that might shelter them. Increasingly, the untamed frontier of Argentina beckoned.

To finance the costly trip and to raise money for them to get a start in South America, Butch hit the Union Pacific train on August 29, 1900, as it neared Tipton, Wyoming. He and Curry forced the engineer to uncouple the passenger cars from the engine and express car, but when they tried to jump into the express car they were stopped by the same worker who had refused to open the train door at Wilcox—Mr. Woodcock. When the conductor saw how much dynamite

Cassidy placed to blow the door, however, he convinced the obstinate Woodcock to open up.

Gang members leapt inside, piled dynamite near the safe, then moved out of range and waited for the explosion. Once again, too much explosive practically disintegrated the safe and propelled its contents about the countryside. After frantically chasing down whatever contents remained intact, the gang robbed the passengers and departed.

The money taken from Tipton was not enough to support Butch Cassidy's plans for South America, so he selected another target that he hoped would be more profitable. That would not be as easy as before, since local lawmen, as well as the special posse formed by the Union Pacific and led by Joe LeFors, constantly prowled the countryside. Leaving Wyoming, Cassidy guided the gang southwest to Winnemuca, Nevada, and its First National Bank.

On September 19, 1900, Cassidy, Sundance, and three others walked into the bank just as its president, Tom Nixon, was stuffing $32,000 into a wheat sack. Butch jumped over a railing separating customers from Nixon's desk, leveled a pistol at the startled bank officer, and gruffly demanded the money.

When Nixon handed over the cash, Butch and his companions rushed outside, where an elderly couple started yelling "Robbers! Robbers!" Sundance fired a few shots at their feet to scare the pair, and as they scurried out of sight, the woman called back to Sundance "don't shoot Pa, he won't hurt you-uns."

Escaping amid a flurry of gunfire, the outlaws barely eluded three posses, especially one that formed in a neighboring town when it had been quickly notified by telephone of the rob-

Many members of Butch Cassidy's gang died violently. Former Hole-In-The-Wall gang members Ben Kilpatrick and Old Beck were killed in 1912 during an attempted train robbery in Texas.

bery. The lawmen hotly pursued the gang for three days, but Cassidy and the rest escaped and headed for the safety of Fort Worth, Texas.

While living much of their lives on the edge of death and constantly on guard lest they be captured, the Wild Bunch blundered drastically in Fort Worth by walking into a clothing store, purchasing derby hats and suits as a joke, and walking over to John Schwartz's photography gallery for a group picture. The famous photograph shows Butch and Sundance, along with Bill Carver, Ben Kilpatrick, and Kid Curry, posing like any normal businessmen might for a company picture.

However, they were not normal businessmen, and though they may have enjoyed sitting for the image, the law had the final laugh. Schwartz liked the photograph so much that, hoping to draw in more customers, he enlarged it and placed it in his store window. A few weeks later a Pinkerton agent walked by and recognized some of the men in the picture. Copies of the photo were made, and soon pictures of Butch and Sundance adorned every lawman's office in the West. No longer was it safe for them to remain in the country.

In February 1901 Cassidy, Sundance, and Sundance's girlfriend, Etta Place, arrived in New York City with the intention of purchasing tickets aboard a steamship for South America. Posing as cattlemen and using false names, they spent three weeks shopping and enjoying the sights of the sprawling city, including stopping at Tiffany's to purchase a gold watch for Etta.

While in New York, Cassidy received a letter from Kid Curry asking for his help in yet another robbery. Figuring the extra money would come in handy in Argentina, Cassidy headed west while in March 1901 Longbaugh and Etta, alias Mr. & Mrs. Harry A. Place, steamed for South America on the liner *Herminius*. Butch planned to rejoin his comrades after completing the theft.

On July 3, 1901, Cassidy rode with the Wild Bunch for the final time when the gang held up the Great Northern Coast Flyer. Curry boarded the train as a passenger, and as it neared Wagner, Montana, he stepped toward the train's front. At gunpoint, he ordered the engineer to pull the train over a bridge where Cassidy and the other gang members waited. After blowing open the safe with dynamite, the gang rode off with at least $40,000. Butch Cassidy took his share, traveled to New York, purchased a liner ticket, and headed to Argentina.

He fled at the right time, for lawmen and Pinkerton agents were closing in on the gang. Posses hunted down and killed gang members Bill Carver, Lonny Logan, Flat-Nose George Curry, and Blackjack Ketchum. On a visit to Nashville, Tennessee, Deaf Charley Hanks barely escaped after attempting to use some of the stolen money from the Wagner heist. He fled to San Antonio, Texas, and died in a shootout on April 17, 1902. St. Louis, Missouri, police arrested Ben Kilpatrick, the Tall Texan, when he foolishly spent some of the Wagner money. After serving a lengthy term in the penitentiary, Kilpatrick returned to his life of crime and was killed during a 1912 train robbery.

One of Butch Cassidy's closest cohorts, Kid Curry, fell prey to his violent temper in a Knoxville saloon on December 13, 1901. Angered while playing pool, Curry beat up three men, started destroying the saloon, then shot two policemen who rushed in to stop him. Arrested three days later by pursuing lawmen, Curry eventually received a 25 year term in an Ohio federal prison, broke out, robbed another train, and died in 1904 when a posse cornered him in Colorado.

Elza Lay met a better fate than the others. After serving his prison term Lay married and lived quietly in Wyoming, content to read and conduct geological work in the West.

The Wild Bunch was no more. Between 1889 and 1901 the gang staged nine major heists in which they stole a total of more than $200,000—almost $2.5 million in today's money. As with most bandits, though, they paid heavily for their actions. By the time Butch Cassidy and the Sundance Kid settled down in Argentina, most of the gang had been killed or imprisoned. While Butch and Sundance remained free, it was only a matter of time before the law closed in on them, too.

"They Seem Like Such Nice People"

While Butch Cassidy assaulted the Great Northern one last time in the United States, the Sundance Kid and Etta Place purchased a huge ranch in Argentina and waited for Cassidy to join them. After the couple arrived in Buenos Aires, Longbaugh deposited $12,000 in the London River Platte Bank. For the next two weeks the two acted like typical American travelers, staying at the plush Hotel Europa, wearing fine clothes, and eating in the best restaurants.

They disappeared almost as quickly as they arrived in Buenos Aires. Longbaugh used part of the money to buy a spread in a remote section of Chubut Province 950 miles southwest of Buenos Aires. The locale perfectly suited their needs, since it could only be reached after a difficult trip through thick jungles, sat in terrain that reminded Longbaugh of the American Rock-

Etta Place traveled to Brazil with the Sundance Kid to avoid the law. There, they bought a ranch and waited for Butch to join them.

–43–

ies, and was ideal for raising cattle and other animals. Their new home appeared to be about as far from the reach of modern law enforcement agencies as could be found, although a few other Americans lived in the general area. As one person described it, that part of Argentina "was a pretty wild place, large enough to swallow up an army without leaving a trace."

One man, John C. Perry, a former sheriff from Texas, suspected his new neighbors were outlaws but, as most people did in that isolated portion of South America, he kept to his own business as long as his neighbors caused no trouble. Texas cattleman Jarred Jones and New York dentist George Newberry, who lived in Buenos Aires as the United States vice consul, also owned ranches in the province.

Butch Cassidy rejoined his friends in April 1902. While he remained on the ranch to stock it with 1,300 sheep, 500 cattle, and 35 horses, Longbaugh and Place returned to New York for a brief visit for medical purposes, then steamed back to Argentina in July.

The trip home proved costly. Soon after Longbaugh and Place left New York, Pinkerton agents picked up their trail. While the company alerted all its offices that the wanted trio resided somewhere in Argentina, for some unexplained reason they did not notify police in that country, who could have easily arrested the Sundance Kid as he stepped off the liner from New York.

In early March 1903 the Pinkerton Agency shifted one of its key operatives, Frank Dimaio, from Brazil to Buenos Aires with the instructions to locate and arrest Butch Cassidy and the Sundance Kid. He first checked with the United States Legation in Buenos Aires to compile a list of any Americans residing in the country. When he showed photographs of the fugitives to Dr. Newberry, the dentist readily identified them as his new neighbors in Chubut Province, but he knew them by different names.

"Harry Place [Sundance Kid] and Jim Ryan [Butch Cassidy] are good fellows," added Newberry. "They have improved their ranch and doubled their stock within the past year. Mrs. Place is a very pretty woman."

When Dimaio told Newberry that his neighbors were ruthless criminals from back home, he reacted with astonishment. "I can't believe they are robbers. They seem like such nice people."

Dimaio wanted to travel out to Chubut Province immediately, but the narrow, bumpy jungle and mountainous trails were washed out by the rainy season then in progress. The trip out would be difficult enough in superb weather, for Dimao would first have to take a steamer 250 miles south, then hire a guide and purchase supplies for a two to three week trip through challenging terrain. Instead, he distributed 150 "Wanted" posters throughout the area. The posters were printed in Spanish and pictured the three outlaws.

Dimaio's other duties kept him from concentrating only on this case, but word filtered to Cassidy that someone had learned the location of their hideout and had flooded the Buenos Aires region with their photographs. He knew it was simply a matter of time before lawmen appeared at the ranch. In 1906 the three returned to robbing banks and living on the run, in part because of Dimaio's pressure but also because they had by now familiarized themselves with Argentina and were confident the

This photograph of Butch Cassidy, taken when he was arrested in 1894, was circulated in Brazil by detectives and lawmen still searching for the elusive outlaw.

country's banks could be easily hit.

A string of heists unfolded over a one year span from 1906 to 1907, each done by a pair of English-speaking men. Dubbed the Bandidos Yanqui by Argentine authorities and people, the duo popped up, robbed a bank, and quickly disappeared into Argentina's dense interior.

In March 1906, Butch and Sundance entered a bank in Villa Mercedes, a village 500 miles west of Buenos Aires, while Etta remained outside to watch for any intruders. Revolver in hand, Cassidy jumped over a railing and ordered the manager to fill a sack with money. He grabbed the sack from the scared bank official, hurried outside with Sundance, and quickly rode out of town on horses that Etta had guarded.

The duo could hardly believe how simple it was to take the money, in this case $20,000. Though a small posse followed, Butch and Sundance melted into the jungle and easily eluded their pursuers. The duo fell into a pattern of robbing a bank, then splitting up and reuniting later at a predetermined location, most frequently in Santiago, Chile, beyond Argentina's western border.

The three Americans, sometimes accompanied by Argentine collaborators, hopelessly outclassed their Argentine foes. After grabbing $20,000 from a bank in Bahia Blanca, Cassidy stopped one posse by shooting the lead horse. The three robbed a bank in neighboring Bolivia, then returned and hit a bank at Rio Gallegos in southern Argentina.

The Bandidos Yanqui were likely to appear almost anywhere in the region, then blend into the terrain. While police hunted for them in one locale, Butch and Sundance robbed a bank somewhere else. Before long, they enjoyed an almost legendary status among Argentina's poorer citizens.

Cassidy felt so confident that one day he walked into the London River Platte Bank, where he and Sundance kept their money, and asked the manager if he could inspect the vault.

"Why, señor, do you want to see our vaults?" wondered the confused official.

"Well, sir," replied Cassidy, "we've worked hard for this money and we're afraid of robbers."

The manager laughed, then assured his customer, "There are no robbers in Buenos Aires."

One reason Cassidy walked with such confidence was that, as he had in the United States, he took extra pains to win support from the native inhabitants. Percy Siebert, who worked with Cassidy and knew him quite well, wrote that "Cassidy was quite popular in the countryside, particularly with the Indian children. Whenever he went to La Paz he would always come back with sticks of candy which he gave to the children. I can still see him coming up the trail to our place, followed by a pack of yelling, laughing kids, who called him Don Max."

A frustrated agent tracking the outlaw wrote his superiors that his search would always end unsuccessfully because "as soon as Cassidy entered an Indian village he would be playing with the children. When he was hard pressed by the authorities he would always find a hide-out among the native population."

However, as happens to every notorious criminal, Butch Cassidy and the Sundance Kid were living on borrowed time. Sooner or later they would slip or a determined lawman would hunt them down. When the showdown unfolded, it was liable to be bloody.

7

"Not Exactly Angels"

Etta Place was the first of the trio to leave the life of crime. Following what most accounts claim to be appendicitis, Place, with Longbaugh, returned to the United States to seek treatment at a well-known Denver establishment. While the Sundance Kid headed back to South America, Etta's whereabouts after her recovery remain a mystery. She was not heard from again.

In the spring of 1907, Butch Cassidy and the Sundance Kid rode to a mountain tin mine in a remote section of Bolivia, where they were hired as payroll guards. Using the aliases Jim Maxwell (Butch) and Enrique Brown, the two fell into a pattern—they worked at the Concordia Tin Mines for a time, then disappeared for a few weeks during which they hit either a bank or Bolivian train, before riding back to their payroll job.

The mine's assistant manager, Percy Seib-

Harry "Sundance Kid" Longbaugh and Etta Place in Brazil. Etta returned to the United States, leaving Butch and Sundance behind, and was never heard from again.

This photo is believed to be Butch Cassidy; however, some sources claim it is actually a man named Mike Steele, who lived nearby.

ert, related that all the other workers, as well as management, figured that Maxwell and Brown were thieves but did not worry about it. Seibert believed it was none of his business since many characters living in that part of Bolivia owned shady pasts. "It must be recalled that the Bolivian interior of that time was a rugged country and, as in the American west, the law was usually what hung on a man's hip. Questions were never asked about a man's background and information was never volunteered."

Only one point bothered the mine's manager, Clement Rolla Glass. Glass did not care if his new employees robbed a train or bank, as long as they left the Concordia Tin Mines' payroll alone. When a worker informed Glass that he had overheard Butch and Sundance discussing plans to steal the mine payroll, Glass picked up his rifle and stormed over to their bunkhouse.

"Why the hardware, Mr. Glass?" asked a surprised Butch Cassidy when the manager walked into the room.

With an icy glare, Glass replied, "Look, I know you're Cassidy and your partner's Harry Longbaugh. I don't care who you are, but I heard you were planning to rob the mine."

When both Cassidy and Longbaugh denied the charge and claimed they had been discussing a different operation, Glass added, "I'm not a policeman. What I'm concerned about is my mine. I'm responsible for the property, the money and the men who work under me."

Butch Cassidy tried to reassure Glass that they meant no harm to anyone or anything at the Concordia Tin Mines. He emphasized that many of the miners had criminal pasts, but that no one cared about it as long as they did their jobs. "There's a lot of men working under you who are not exactly angels. If they were, they wouldn't be here. Let's leave it like this, Mr. Glass. I'm Maxwell and the Kid is Brown. Don't worry about your mine. The people here are our friends and you've been a good boss. We don't rob people we work for. Is that a deal?"

Satisfied that he had made his point, Glass agreed and turned to walk out. As he stepped near the door he noticed that Sundance, who had been lying on his bunk, was ready to take more severe steps if needed. Though he had been propped up on one elbow the entire time, Glass told Seibert later that "under the blanket I could see the tip of a six-shooter."

Seibert and his wife befriended the outlaws and frequently invited them to dinner. Sundance remained typically quiet most of the time, but Cassidy cracked jokes and tried to make everybody relax. At the dinner table he normally sat at the end that gave him a view through the window of the trail and valley below in case any intruders suddenly appeared, but he kept the suppers interesting with his friendly manner.

Even he, though, experienced his moments of melancholy. "I came down to South America with the idea of settling down," he told Seibert. "In the States there was nothing but jail, the noose, or being shot by a posse. I thought maybe I could change things but I guess things at this late date can't be changed." He then added, with rare sadness, "I know how it's going to end, Perce. I guess that's the way it's got to be."

Cassidy's somber words proved true, although accounts differ as to exactly how he and Sundance met their end, or even if they died in South America. Apparently going against their word to Glass, the two robbed the Chocaya Tin-Silver Mine payroll along a narrow mountain trail. They also took with them a silver-gray mule, branded with the mine's emblem. Angered that the two Americans had turned on the people that had shielded them for so long, local mine owners contacted the police about arresting Cassidy and Longbaugh, and the outlaws were forced to flee the region.

The duo rode into the small town of San Vicente, about 350 miles southeast of La Paz. While the outlaws rested inside a small hut sit-

Great Northern Express Co.

ST. PAUL, MINN., JULY 4, 1901.

$5000 Reward

The Great Northern Railway "Overland" West-bound Train No. 3 was held up about three miles east of Wagner, Mont., Wednesday afternoon, July 3, 1901, and the Great Northern Express Company's through safe blown open with dynamite and the contents taken.

There were three men connected with the hold-up, described as follows:

One was, height 5 feet and 9 inches, weight about 175 pounds, blue eyes, had a projecting brow and about two weeks growth of sandy beard on chin, wore new tan shoes, black coat, corduroy trousers, and carried a silver plated, gold mounted Colt's revolver with a pearl handle.

Second man, height 6 feet, weight about 175 pounds, sandy complexion, blue eyes, not very large with slight cast in left eye; wore workingman's shoes, blue overalls over black suit of clothes, had a boot leg for cartridge pouch suspended from his neck.

Third man resembled a half breed very strongly, had large dark eyes, smoothly shaven face, and a very prominent nose; features clear cut, weight about 180 pounds, slightly stooped in shoulders, but very square across the shoulders, and wore a light slouch hat.

All three men used very marked Texas cowboy dialect, and two of them carried Winchester rifles, one of which was new. One had a carbine, same pattern as the Winchesters. They rode away on black, white, and buckskin horses respectively.

The Great Northern Express Company will give $5000 reward for the capture and identification of the three men, or a proportionate amount for one or two and $500 additional for each conviction.

D. S. ELLIOTT,
Auditor.

Approved:
D. MILLER,
President.

South American authorities, as well as detectives hired by the railroad and bank victims of Butch Cassidy in the United States, would not give up in their quest to find Butch and Sundance. This "Wanted" poster describes the two robbers.

uated in a corral with ten-foot walls, a police officer spotted the mule and alerted other authorities. Quickly, the authorities—depending on the account, as few as three police officers to a large group of police supported by Bolivian soldiers—closed in on the Bandidos Yanquis.

The silence inside the hut was broken when an officer shouted for Cassidy and Longbaugh to surrender. Butch and Sundance answered with gunfire. In an ensuing exchange of shots, one Bolivian was killed. Both Americans knew they could not hold out indefinitely, especially as they had left their rifles and most of the ammunition outside with the pack animals. They had no choice but to rush out under fire, grab the needed weapons, and dash back inside.

The Sundance Kid volunteered to get their rifles. With Butch laying down covering fire with his revolver, Sundance bolted into the opening, dodged bullets that splattered into the ground near his feet, and made it to the mules. Retrieving whatever he could carry, Sundance took a deep breath and sprang once more into the gap between the animals and the hut. Before he reached his destination, though, Sundance spun to the ground from a bullet wound. Butch quickly darted out and started to drag his friend into the hut, but he, too, fell from a Bolivian bullet. Summoning every ounce of strength he still retained, Cassidy crawled back into the hut, dragging Longbaugh behind him.

The gunfight slowed to a stalemate as daylight lessened. The Bolivians were afraid to rush two heavily-armed criminals, while the outlaws realized that any further scamper outside would surely result in their deaths. Later that night, two gunshots rang from inside the hut, yet the Bolivians held their positions until the next morning. When they crashed through the door of the hut, the two lifeless bodies of the Americans lay on the floor. Apparently, Butch shot the badly wounded Sundance Kid with one bullet, then killed himself with the second.

This is where accounts differ. While local inhabitants claimed that the outlaws were buried in an Indian graveyard near San Vicente, one story asserted that Butch Cassidy actually escaped by putting on the uniform of a Bolivian soldier and crawling away under cover of darkness. Bolivian newspapers reported the duo's deaths, and Percy Seibert confirmed that his

friends had died, but the accounts give different years for their demise. Some stories state the Bandidos Yanquis died in 1908, some in 1909, and yet others claim 1912.

A heated debate raged over the following years. An April 23, 1930, article in the Washington Post newspaper proclaimed "BUTCH IS DEAD" and presented arguments, largely based

Although some people said Butch Cassidy was killed in a gun battle in 1908, Pinkerton Agency detectives did not close their file on the bandit until 1921.

upon Percy Seibert, that the infamous outlaws died at San Vicente. However, those who disagreed countered that Seibert never actually saw the corpses, but only assumed the two bodies had to be his friends. Who else could it be, thought Seibert, when he learned that two Americans had been killed after a robbery?

Gradually a story emerged that instead of dying in Bolivia, Butch Cassidy reappeared as William T. Phillips and lived until 1937. Author Larry Pointer concluded in his research for the 1977 book, *In Search of Butch Cassidy*, that Seibert lied about the bodies' identities to help his friend escape. Pointer reported that after the supposed gun battle—of which he could uncover no official record in the Bolivian army archives—Butch fled through thick jungle, boarded a steamer for Paris, France, then traveled to Adrian, Michigan, in 1908, where he married Gertrude Livesay. The couple lived in Arizona and Spokane, Washington, before heading to Alaska, where Cassidy met the famous western marshal, Wyatt Earp. The lawman later claimed that Phillips was indeed Butch Cassidy.

After returning to Spokane, Phillips invented an adding machine and started a successful business called the Phillips Manufacturing Company. His family life apparently prospered as well. In 1919, according to Larry Pointer, the couple adopted a boy and, not long after, moved into a larger house. In 1925 Phillips traveled to his childhood home in Utah, where he had an emotional reunion with his eighty-one-year-old father, Max, and his sister, Lula.

In the 1930s, Phillips turned to odd jobs when his business soured. To ease his financial crunch, he wrote a book about his life as Butch Cassidy called *The Bandit Invincible*, but no publisher would take a chance on the volume since it was so poorly written. The book contained details of events that only Butch Cassidy would know, and a handwriting expert who compared Phillips's scrawl with notes that Cassidy had penned declared they came from the same hand. Disheartened and broke, William Phillips died of cancer in 1937.

The Pinkerton Agency doubted Cassidy's death sufficiently to keep its records on the outlaw open as late as 1921. However, others scoffed at the notion that Cassidy could have escaped the gunfight. In December 1987, two authors who sought a conclusive answer to the riddle, Anne Meadows and Daniel Buck, unearthed new evidence in a stack of old company documents in southern Bolivia. The Aramayo Mine Company records contained a complete account of the payroll robbery, pursuit of the thieves, and gunfight at San Vicente.

According to the frayed pages the mine's manager, Carlos Pero, was transporting the payroll to the mine with his son, Mariano, and a servant on November 3, 1908, when two masked men, heavily armed and draped with ammunition belts, halted them on a lonely mountain trail and took the money. Pero rode to a nearby mining camp to alert his company, then informed local authorities. Quickly an array of police, Bolivian soldiers, and mine workers, angered that their entire month's pay had been lost, set out in pursuit.

On November 7 three Bolivian soldiers, led by a captain, located Cassidy and Longbaugh in San Vicente and engaged in a sharp gun battle. One Bolivian soldier died in the fighting, but the Bolivians killed both American bandits and recovered the payroll. Indian villagers buried the bodies in a single grave in the town cemetery, then placed a padlocked chain around the tombstone to prevent the outlaws' evil spirits from escaping. Meadows and Buck claimed that these records discount Pointer's book, which stated the outlaw left Bolivia one year before the actual struggle at San Vicente, and proved that Butch Cassidy died in the jungles of Bolivia.

As a result of the paradox of Cassidy's life and the uncertainty of his death, the legend of Butch Cassidy has grown over the years. An award-winning 1969 movie starring Paul Newman and Robert Redford, *Butch Cassidy and the Sundance Kid*, added to the legend. The movie protrayed Butch as a likeable, carefree individual who simply happened to steal money.

Whatever final fate Cassidy actually met, no doubt should exist about his life, however. Though he may have been a friendly individual, he devoted his years to a life of crime that hurt other people physically, emotionally, and financially. Rather than a hero, the criminal was no better than any other villain who illegally profited from the work of others.

The Pinkerton agent who searched for Butch Cassidy in Argentina, Frank Dimaio, later stated the issue with appropriate bluntness:

> Today the outlaws of the West, like Cassidy, are viewed through the eyes of romance, but on the frontier stealing a herd of horses was like a modern gang stealing a carload of cars. A horse was an important means of a man's transportation in a wild land, and that's what Butch Cassidy was stealing before he could vote.
>
> He was also a rustler, and in the Wild West that meant he was stealing another man's bread and butter. From a horse thief and rustler he graduated to robbing banks and trains. I've heard the old

stories of how Cassidy never killed a man until he reached South America, but does that make him a better man? We must consider he was riding stirrup-to-stirrup with Harvey Logan, the most deadly killer in the West, and it took very little to make Logan go for his gun. Even in the old West the law was specific: if an express messenger was killed during the commission of a holdup, not only the man who fired the shot was responsible but also his companions who took part in the commission of that felonious robbery.

So when Cassidy reached South America he was a seasoned criminal, a horse thief, rustler, bank and train robber.

That is his legacy, and that is how Robert Leroy Parker, alias Butch Cassidy, should be remembered.

CHRONOLOGY

1866   Robert Leroy Parker is born in Beaver, Utah, on April 13

1884   Parker admits to stealing horses, then leaves Beaver,
       changing his last name to Cassidy in honor of his friend,
       Mike Cassidy

1889   Cassidy and the McCarty Gang rob the First National Bank in
       Denver, Colorado, on March 30. On June 24, he hits the San Miguel
       Valley Bank in Telluride, Colorado

1890   Cassidy works as a butcher, earning the nickname "Butch," after the
       McCarty gang breaks up

1892   Butch Cassidy is arrested by Deputy Sheriff Bob Calverly on April 8.
       In the next year, he stands trial for stealing horses and is found
       guilty. He is sentenced to two years hard labor at the Laramie City,
       Wyoming, penitentiary

1896   After his release from prison, Cassidy forms the the Wild Bunch. The
       gang robs a Montpelier, Idaho, bank on August 13

1897   Cassidy and Lay rob the Denver & Rio Grande train on April 21

1899   Cassidy holds up the Union Pacific's Overland Flyer at Wilcox,
       Wyoming, on June 2. The Wild Bunch steals $30,000 near Folsom,
       New Mexico, on July 11. The gang's robbery spree forces the Union
       Pacific Railroad to hire the Pinkerton National Detective Agency to
       stop the gang

1900   The Wild Bunch robs the Union Pacific train near Tipton, Wyoming,
       on August 29. In September, the gang strikes at the First National
       Bank in Winnemuca, Nevada

1901   Butch Cassidy and the Sundance Kid conduct their final raid with
       The Wild Bunch on July 3, holding up a train in Montana

1902   Cassidy, Harry Longbaugh, and Etta Place move to Argentina in
       April

1903   Frank Dimaio is assigned to track down the three outlaws

1906   Butch Cassidy and the Sundance Kid return to robbing banks

1907   Butch and Sundance work at the Concordia Tin Mines

1908   The gun battle at San Vicente, in which Cassidy and Sundance are supposedly killed, occurs

1937   William T. Phillips, who claimed he was Butch Cassidy and had escaped death at San Vicente, dies from cancer

1969   The movie *Butch Cassidy and the Sundance Kid* premiers, adding to the legend about the outlaws

1987   Writers Anne Meadows and Daniel Buck discover evidence of Butch Cassidy's death at San Vicente in 1908

FURTHER READING

Hamilton, John. *Butch Cassidy*. Minneapolis: Abdo & Daughters, 1996.

Horan, James D. *The Authentic Wild West: The Outlaws*. New York: Crown Publishers, Inc., 1977.

Kelly, Charles. *The Outlaw Trail: A History of Butch Cassidy and His Wild Bunch*. New York: Bonanza Books, 1938.

Meadows, Anne and Daniel Buck. Running down a Legend. *Americas* 42 (1991): 21-27.

Metz, Leon Claire. *The Shooters*. New York: Berkley Books, 1976.

O'Neal, Bill. *Encyclopedia of Western Gunfighters*. Norman: University of Oklahoma Press, 1979.

Pointer, Larry. *In Search of Butch Cassidy*. Norman: University of Oklahoma Press, 1977.

Rennert, Vincent Paul. *Western Outlaws*. New York: Crowell-Collier Press, 1968.

Trachtman, Paul. *The Old West: The Gunfighters*. New York: Time-Life Books, 1974.

INDEX

PICTURE CREDITS

ABOUT THE AUTHOR

John F. Wukovits is a teacher and writer from Trenton, Michigan. His work has appeared in more than 25 national publications, including *Wild West* and *America's Civil War.* His books include a biography of the World War II commander Admiral Clifton Sprague, and he has written biographies of Barry Sanders, Jesse James, and Wyatt Earp for Chelsea House. A graduate of the University of Notre Dame, Wukovits is the father of three daughters—Amy, Julie, and Karen.